the **English** Springer Spaniel

A guide to selection, care, nutrition, upbringing, training, health, breeding, sports and play

about pets

Contents

Foreword

The book you are holding right now is by no means a complete book about the English Springer Spaniel. If we had collected all the information about the breed, its history and development, feeding, training, health, and whatever else there is to know, this book would have consisted of at least five hundred pages.

What we have done, however, is to bring together all the basic information that you as a (future) owner of an English Springer Spaniel need to know in order to handle your pet responsibly. Unfortunately, there are still people who buy a pet without thinking through what they are about to get into.

This book generally deals with the history of the English Springer Spaniel, the breed standard and the advantages and disadvantages of buying a dog of this breed. It also contains essential information about feeding and about the very first steps in training your dog. Reproduction, day-to-day care, and health and breed-specific illnesses are also topics.

After having read this book, you can make a carefully considered decision to buy an English Springer Spaniel and to keep it as a pet in a responsible manner. We advise you, however, not to rely on this book only. A well-reared and trained dog is more than just a dog. Invest therefore in a puppy training course or an obedience course. There are also plenty of excellent books that deal with certain aspects for which we do not have the space in this small book.

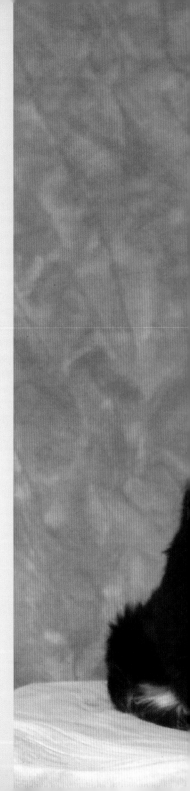

about pets

A Publication of About Pets.

All rights reserved, including the right
to reproduce this book or portions
thereof in any form whatsoever.

Copyright © 2006
About Pets
co-publisher United Kingdom
Kingdom Books
PO9 5TL, England

ISBN 185279190X
First printed Januar 2005
Second revised printing Januar 2006

Original title: de Engelse Springer spaniel
© 2004-2006 Welzo Media Productions
bv,
About Pets bv,
Warffum, the Netherlands
www.aboutpets.info

Photos: Kingdom books,
Isabelle Francoiise, Rob Dekker,
Jeanne van Beers and Helma van de
Brink

Printed in China

The English Springer Spaniel is one of the oldest breeds of all hunting spaniels. Its original task was to track down game and to drive it into nets, towards falcons or greyhounds.

This is also where this breed gets its name from: 'springing the game' means to drive game out of hiding. At present the English Springer is still used as a gundog that tracks down and drives out game and retrieves it when shot. This friendly, tolerant dog is also very well suited as a companion, as long as it gets plenty of exercise and attention.

History
According to Toepoel's Dog Encyclopaedia, the origin of this breed lies in continental Europe. Especially France and Spain are often referred to in this respect. The English Springer Spaniel became widely spread across England later on. English Springer Spaniels can already be seen on paintings from 1625, by the Dutch artist Jan Steen. In that era, the Springer was a first-class gundog. It was bred in the colours brown, orange or red with white. It measured approximately two-fifths of the size of the Setter. In around 1902, the first English Springer Spaniels appeared at dog shows in England. Hunters often consider the present-day show dog as too heavy and big. They regard mobility and speed as very important characteristics. The first official register for the English Springer Spaniel was opened in England in 1902.

In general

Character

The English Springer Spaniel is an intelligent gundog that is very mobile. It is inexhaustible and loves going for long walks in the countryside. It has always been bred to track birds and drive them out of the undergrowth. When taking your English Springer for walks, you will notice that even today's dogs are very curious and alert. They have a very strong passion for hunting: English Springers are always ready to hunt down 'game' in shrubs and parks. Due to its intelligence, the English Springer Spaniel needs a rigorous upbringing. It learns very quickly and this is both an advantage and a disadvantage. Once it notices that it can get away with something or escape somewhere it will always try again. Thus do not give up too easily when teaching your dog to have its coat groomed or its nails clipped.

Your English Springer loves challenges and will love working for you. Do not let your dog sit at home without giving it some work to do. In the case of the English Springer, boredom can lead to vandalism! Try to be active with your dog: go and participate in dog sports with it or train it for dog shows. Your English Springer has a strong desire to please you. English Springer Spaniels are very happy dogs, and they greet every visitor with the same enthusiasm. If you are looking for a guard dog or do not have the time to take your dog for lots of long walks, you should look at other breeds.

UK Kennel Club and their breed standards

What does the UK Kennel Club? To say it in their own words: "The Kennel Club is committed to developing and supporting a nation of responsible dog owners. As well as organising events and campaigns to help dog owners meet their responsibilities, the Kennel Club also produces a range of literature to assist the dog owning public."

What is the use of a Breed Standard? The Kennel clubs answer: "The basis of breed shows is the judging of dogs against the 'Breed Standard', which is the prescribed blueprint of the particular breed of dog. For all licensed breed shows, the Kennel Club Breed Standards must be used for the judging of dogs." More about the UK Kennel Club Breed Standards: "The Breed Standards are owned by the Kennel Club, and all changes are subject to approval by the Kennel Club General Committee. New Breed Standards, for newly recognised breeds, are drawn up once the breed has become sufficiently established within the UK. Careful research is conducted into the historical background, health and temperament of any new breed before Kennel Club recognition is granted. The Kennel Club currently recognises 196 breeds. Upon recognition, breeds are placed on the Imported Breed Register until

In general

they are deemed eligible for transferral to the Breed Register".

A standard provides a guideline for breeders and judges. It is something of an ideal that dogs of each breed must strive to match. With some breeds, dogs are already being bred that match the ideal. Other breeds have a long way to go. There is a list of defects for each breed. These can be serious defects that disqualify the dog, in which case it will be excluded from breeding. Permitted defects are not serious, but do cost points in a show.

The UK Kennel Club Breed Standard for the English Springer Spaniel

General Appearance
Of all British land spaniels, this is the fastest and the one with the longest legs.
Symmetrically built, compact, strong, merry, active. Highest on leg and raciest in build of all British land spaniels.

Characteristics
Breed is of ancient and pure origins, oldest of sporting gundogs; original purpose was finding and springing game for net, falcon or greyhound. Now used to find, flush and retrieve game for gun.

Temperament
Friendly, happy disposition, biddable. Timidity or aggression highly undesirable.

Head and Skull
Skull of medium length, fairly broad, slightly rounded, rising from foreface, making a brow or stop, divided by fluting between eyes, dying away along forehead towards occipital bone which should not be prominent. Cheeks flat. Foreface of proportionate length to skull, fairly broad and deep, well chiselled below eyes, fairly deep and square in flew. Nostrils well developed.

Eyes
Medium size, almond-shaped, not prominent nor sunken, well set in (not showing haw), alert, kind expression. Dark hazel. Light eyes undesirable.

Ears
Lobular, good length and width, fairly close to head, set in line with eye. Nicely feathered.

Mouth
Jaws strong, with a perfect, regular and complete scissor bite, i.e. upper teeth closely overlapping lower teeth and set square to the jaws.

Neck
Good length, strong and muscular, free from throatiness, slightly arched, tapering towards head.

Forequarters
Forelegs straight and well boned. Shoulders sloping and well laid. Elbows set well to body. Strong flexible pasterns.

the **English Springer Spaniel**

Body
Strong, neither too long nor too short. Chest deep, well developed. Well sprung ribs. Loin muscular, strong with slight arch and well coupled.

Hindquarters
Hindlegs well let down. Stifles and hocks moderately bent. Thighs broad, muscular, well developed. Coarse hocks undesirable.

Feet
Tight, compact, well rounded, with strong, full pads.

Tail
Customarily docked.
Docked: Set low, never carried above level of back. Well feathered with lively action.
Undocked: Set low, never carried above level of back. Well feathered with lively action. In balance with the rest of the dog.

Gait/Movement
Strictly his own. Forelegs swing straight forward from shoulder, throwing feet well forward in an easy free manner. Hocks driving well under body, following in line with forelegs. At slow movement may have a pacing stride typical of this breed.

Coat
Close, straight and weather resisting, never coarse. Moderate feathering on ears, forelegs, body and hindquarters.

Colour
Liver and white, black and white, or either of these colours with tan markings.

Size
Approximate height: 51 cm (20 in).

Faults
Any departure from the foregoing points should be considered a fault and the seriousness with which the fault should be regarded should be in exact proportion to its degree and its effect upon the health and welfare of the dog.

Note
Male animals should have two apparently normal testicles fully descended into the scrotum.
July 2001

Reproduced with courtesy of the Kennel Club of Great Britain,

Buying your English Springer Spaniel

Once you made that properly considered decision to buy a dog, you have various options. Do you want a puppy, an adult dog, or even an older dog? Would you rather have a bitch or a dog, a pedigree dog or a cross?

Of course, the question also arises as to where to get your dog; from a private person, a reliable breeder, or from an animal shelter? It is important for you and the animal that you sort out all these things in advance, as you want to make sure that you get a dog that suits your circumstances.

With a puppy, you choose a playful, energetic housemate that finds it easy to adapt to its new environment. If you prefer things a bit quieter, an older dog is a good choice.

Advantages and disadvantages

The English Springer Spaniel was originally bred as a gundog. It has been bred with a focus on ensuring a good and cooperative character. The Springer has an enormous will to please, and it will do anything it can to fulfil your wishes. It is a trusty and loyal companion. Its pleasantly soft coat makes the English Springer Spaniel a dog that is nice to cuddle. It is also intelligent, sociable and very active. If you are a sporty person who enjoys long walks or if you would like to do sports with your dog, then the English Springer Spaniel is the right breed for you. English Springer Spaniels are not

excessive barkers.

There are also disadvantages to keeping a gundog as a pet. The English Springer Spaniel still has a very strong hunting instinct. It needs to be brought up rigorously by a knowledgeable person. If you live in a flat or in the centre of town, then an active dog such as the English Springer Spaniel is not a good choice for you. It is a dog that needs a lot of exercise. The Springer is also very easily distracted, as game could be hiding behind every bush. It is also mad about water and will not be able to resist any ditches or ponds you come across on your walks. The Springer's long coat is weather resistant, but also needs a lot of care.

What are your plans?

Another question you need to answer for yourself if you are planning to buy an English Springer Spaniel is: do you want a dog to go hunting with and/or do dog sports with, do you want a show dog or just a pet? At

the **English Springer Spaniel**

present, a split can be seen in the lineage of the breed. Show dogs have increased in size. The real hunting dog still has a very strongly developed hunting instinct and still needs more exercise than a show dog. Crosses between these two lines are often described as dogs from a dual-purpose line, i.e. dogs that are suitable both as gundogs and as show dogs.

Also think about the following before you decide on your future dog. Do you have a preferred coat colour, for example? The dog also needs to fit into your family situation. If you have children, you should choose a more softly natured puppy instead of a dominant one. Clearly explain your wishes to the breeder, as he is the person most able to help you choose the right puppy. This can prevent a lot of disappointment.

Male or female?

Whether you choose a male or a female puppy, or an adult dog or bitch, is an entirely personal decision. A male typically needs more leadership because he tends to be more dominant by nature. He will try to play boss over other dogs and, if he gets the chance, over people too. In the wild, the most dominant dog (or wolf) is always the leader of the pack. In many cases this is a male. A bitch is usually much more focussed on her master, as she sees him as the pack leader.

A puppy test is good for defining what kind of character a young dog will develop. During a test one usually sees that a dog is more dominant than a bitch. You can often quickly recognise the bossy, the adventurous and the cautious characters. So visit the litter a couple of times early on. Try to pick a puppy that suits your own personality. A dominant dog, for instance, needs a strong hand. It will often try to see how far it can go. You must regularly make it clear who's the boss, and that it must obey all the members of the family.

When bitches are sexually mature, they will go into season. On average, a bitch is in season twice a year for about two to three weeks. This is the fertile period when she can mate. Particularly in the second half of her season, she will want to go looking for a dog to mate with, and she can be covered in this time. A dog will show more masculine traits once he is sexually mature. He will make sure other dogs know what territory is his by urinating as often as possible in as many places as he can. He will also be difficult to restrain if there's a bitch in season nearby. As far as general care is concerned, there is little difference between a dog and a bitch.

Puppy or adult?

After you've decided on a male or a female, the next question comes up. Should it be a puppy or an adult dog? Your household circumstances usually play a major role here.

Of course, it's great having a sweet little puppy in the house, but bringing up a young dog takes a lot of time. In its first year it learns more than during the rest of its life. This is the period when the foundations are laid for elementary matters, such as house-training, obedience and social behaviour. You must reckon with the fact that your puppy will keep you busy for a couple of hours a day, certainly in the first few months. You won't need so much time with a grown dog. It has already been brought up, but this doesn't mean it doesn't need correcting from time to time.

A puppy will no doubt leave a trail of destruction in its wake for the first few months. With a little bad luck, this will cost you some rolls of wallpaper, some good shoes and a few socks. In the worst case you'll be left with some chewed furniture. Some puppies even manage to tear curtains from their rails. With good upbringing this 'vandalism' will quickly disappear, but you won't have to worry about this if you get an older dog. The greatest advantage of buying a puppy, of course, is that you can bring it up your own way. And the upbringing a dog gets (or doesn't get) is a major influence on its whole character.

Finally, financial aspects may play a role in your decision. A puppy is generally (much) more expensive than an adult dog, not only in purchase price but also in 'maintenance'. A puppy needs to go to the vet's more often for the necessary vaccinations and check-ups.

Overall, bringing up a puppy requires a good deal of energy, time and money, but you have its upbringing in your own hands. An adult dog costs less money and energy, but its character has already been formed. You should also try to find out about the background of an adult dog. Its previous owner may have formed its character in somewhat less positive ways.

Adult ...

... or puppy?

Two dogs?

Having two or more dogs in the house is not just nice for us, but also for the animals themselves. Dogs get a lot of pleasure from company of their own kind. After all, they are pack animals.

If you're sure that you want two young dogs, it's best not to buy them at the same time. Bringing a dog up and establishing the bond between dog and master takes time, and you need to give a lot of attention to your dog in this phase. Having two puppies in the house means you have to divide your attention between them too much. Apart from that, there's a danger that they will focus on one another rather than on their master. Buy the second pup when the first is (almost) an adult.

Two adult dogs can normally be brought into the house together quite easily as long as they know each other. If this is not the case, then you need to give them the opportunity to get to know each other. This is best achieved by letting the dogs get to know each other on neutral ground. This way you will avoid that one of the dogs will try to defend its territory. On neutral territory, e.g. an acquaintance's garden where neither dog has been before, both dogs are basically equal. Once they got to know each other, you can take them home where they can sort out the hierarchy amongst themselves.

Do not be tempted to intervene in 'squabbles'. This is a human urge, but for the dog higher up in the hierarchy it is as if its position is being undone. This will cause it to display even more dominant behaviour with all the nasty consequences. Once the hierarchy has been established, most dogs will usually get along very well.

Getting a puppy when the first dog is somewhat older often has a positive effect on the older dog. The influence of the puppy almost seems to give it a second childhood. The older dog, if it's been well brought up, can help with the upbringing of the puppy, as young dogs like to imitate the behaviour of their elders. Don't forget to give both dogs the same amount of attention. Take them both for separate walks at least once per day during the first

eighteen months. Make sure the older dog has enough opportunities to get some peace and quiet. It won't always be able to keep up with the speed of such an enthusiastic youngster. A puppy also needs to sleep a lot and thus might need to have the brakes put on once in a while.

The combination of dog and bitch needs special attention. It is advisable to get two dogs of the same sex, as this will prevent a lot of problems. Sterilisation or castration is, of course, a solution to prevent unwanted offspring, but it is a final one. A castrated or sterilised animal will never be able to reproduce again.

A dog and children

English Springers and children are a great combination. They can play together and get great pleasure out of each other's company. Moreover, children need to learn how to handle living beings; they develop a sense of responsibility by caring for a dog (or another pet).

However sweet a dog is, children must understand that it is an animal and not a toy. A dog isn't comfortable when it's being messed around with. It can become frightened, nervous and even aggressive. So make it clear what a dog likes and what it doesn't. Look for ways the child can play with the dog, perhaps a game of hide-and-seek where the child hides and the dog has to find it. Even a simple tennis ball can give enormous pleasure. Children must learn to leave a dog in peace when it doesn't want to play any more. The dog must also have its own place where it's not disturbed. Let your children help with your dog's care as much as possible. A strong bond will be the result.

The arrival of a baby also means changes in the life of a dog. Before the birth you can help to get the dog acquainted with the new situation. Let it sniff at the new things in the house and it will quickly accept them. When the baby has arrived, involve the dog in day-by-day events as much as possible, but make sure it gets plenty of attention too.

Never leave a dog alone with young children! Crawling infants sometimes make unexpected movements, which can easily frighten a dog. Infants are also hugely curious, and may try to find out whether the tail is really fastened to the dog, or whether its eyes come out, just like they do with their cuddly toys. But a dog is a dog and it will defend itself when it feels threatened.

Where to buy your Springer
There are various ways of acquiring an English Springer Spaniel. The decision for a puppy or an adult dog will also determine to a great extent where you buy your dog.

If it is to be a puppy, you need to find a reliable breeder with a litter. If you choose a popular breed such as the English Springer Spaniel, you will have plenty of choice. This also means, however, that you will come across dogs that have only been bred for profit's sake. You can see how many puppies are for sale by looking in the classified section of your local newspaper every Saturday. Some of these dogs have pedigrees, but many don't. When such dogs are bred, breeders also often do not look out for breed-specific illnesses

and in-breeding. The puppies are taken away from their mother as soon as possible and are thus insufficiently socialised. Never buy a puppy which is too young and of which you did not get to see the mother and/or the papers.

Luckily, there are plenty of bona-fide breeders of English Springer Spaniels in the UK. Try to visit several breeders before buying a puppy. It is quite normal that the breeder will ask you about your domestic circumstances in quite a detailed manner, and also about your ideas concerning bringing up and keeping an English Springer Spaniel. A good breeder will try to make sure that all his puppies go to a good home and the right people. Also find out if the breeder is willing to help you after you have bought the puppy and to help you look for solutions if problems should arise.

Finally, you must realise that a pedigree is nothing more or less than a proof of descent. The Kennel Club also issues pedigrees to the young of parents that suffer from congenital conditions, or that have never been checked for them. A pedigree says nothing about the health of the parent dogs.

If you would rather buy an adult dog, you can contact one of the breed associations. They sometimes help with re-homing adult dogs that can no longer be kept by their owners due to circumstances (such as impulse buying, moving home or divorce). The breed associations also help their members with advice before buying a puppy or even importing animals from abroad.

What to watch out for

Buying a puppy is no simple matter. You must pay attention to the following:
- Never buy a puppy on impulse, even if it is love at first sight. A dog is a living being that will need a lot of care and attention over a period of approximately thirteen years (and sometimes even longer). It is not a toy that you can put away when you're done with it.
- Take a good look at the mother. Is she calm, nervous, aggressive, well cared for or neglected? The behaviour and condition of the mother is not only a sign of the quality of the breeder, but also of the puppy you're about to buy.
- Avoid buying a puppy whose mother has been kept in a kennel only. A young dog needs as many different impressions as possible during its first few months, including living in a family. It gets used to people and possibly other pets this way.

Kennel dogs miss these experiences and are inadequately socialised.
- Always ask to see the parents' papers (vaccination certificates, pedigrees, official health examination certificates). A sincere breeder will not have a problem with showing you these papers.
- English Springer Spaniels need to have been checked for Hip Dysplasia (HD). Both parent animals also need to be free of eye abnormalities, such as Progressive Retina Atrophy (PRA), Cataracts and Retina Dysplasia (RD).
- Never buy a puppy younger than eight weeks.
- Put all agreements with the breeder in writing. A model agreement is available from any breed association.

If you would like to take your English Springer Spaniel on holidays with you, there are a few things you need to bear in mind. Even if some dogs do enjoy travelling, there a lot that definitely don't.

If you enjoy travelling to far-away places on your holidays, you need to ask yourself whether your dog will really enjoy it too.

That very first trip

The first trip of a puppy's life is also the most nerve-wrecking. This is the trip from the breeder's to its new home. If possible, pick up your puppy in the morning. It then has the whole day to get used to its new situation. Ask the breeder not to feed the puppy that day. The young animal will be overwhelmed by all kinds of new experiences. Firstly, it's away from its mother; it's in a small room (the car) with all its different smells, noises and strange people. So there's a big chance that the puppy will be carsick this first time, with the annoying consequence that it will remember travelling in the car as an unpleasant experience.

It's thus important to make this first trip as pleasant as possible. When picking up your puppy, always take someone with you who can sit in the back seat with the puppy on his or her lap and talk to it calmly. If it's too warm for the puppy, a place on the floor at the feet of your companion is ideal. The pup will lie there relatively quietly and may even take a nap. Ask the breeder for a cloth or something else that has been lying in the puppies' nest and thus carries the familiar scent. The puppy can lie on this in the car, and it will also help if it feels lonely during the first nights at home.

If the trip home is a long one, then stop for a break (once in a while). Let your puppy roam and sniff around (on the lead!), offer it a little drink of water and, if necessary, let it do its business. Do take care to lay an old towel in the car. It can happen that the puppy, in its nervousness, may urinate or be sick. It's also good advice to let your puppy make positive experiences with car journeys as soon as possible. Make short trips to nice places where you can walk and play with it. It can be a real nuisance if your dog doesn't like travelling in a car. There will always be times when you need to take your dog somewhere in the car, for example to the vet's or to visit family and friends.

Taking your English Springer Spaniel on holidays

When making holiday plans, you also need to think about what you're going to do with your dog during that time. Are you taking it with you, putting it into kennels or leaving it with friends? In any event there are a number of things you need to do in good time.

If you want to take your dog with you, you need to be sure in

advance that it will be welcome at your holiday destination, and what the rules there are. If travelling to foreign countries, your dog will need certain vaccinations and a health certificate, which normally need to be done four weeks before departure. You must also be sure that you've made all the arrangements necessary to bring your dog back home to the UK, without it needing to go into quarantine under the rabies regulations. Your vet can give you the most recent information. If your trip is to southern Europe, ask for a treatment against ticks (you can read more about this in the "Parasites" chapter).

Although you might like the idea of taking your dog on holidays with you, you need to ask yourself honestly if your pet enjoys it as much. English Springers won't enjoy travelling to a hot country, as they don't cope well with heat. Travelling in the car for days is also not normally their preference. Some dogs suffer badly from carsickness. There are good treatments available, but you need to ask yourself whether you are really doing your dog a favour with them.

If you do decide to take your dog with you, make regular stops at safe places during your journey, as your dog needs to have a good run once in a while. Take plenty of fresh drinking water with you, as well as enough of the food your dog is used to. Don't leave your dog in the car standing in the sun. It can quickly be overcome by the heat, which can have fatal consequences. If you really cannot avoid it, park the car in the shade as far as possible and open a window a bit for fresh air. Even if you have taken these precautions: Never stay away long!

If you are travelling by plane or ship, you need to inform yourself well in advance whether your dog is allowed to go with you and what rules apply. Allow plenty of time for your preparations, so that you can find an alternative if necessary.

Maybe you decide not to take your dog with you, and you then need to find somewhere for it to stay. Arrangements for a place in kennels need to be made well in advance. Certain vaccinations will be required, which need to be given a minimum of one month before the stay. If your dog can't be accommodated in the homes of relatives or friends, it might be possible to have an acquaintance stay in your house. This also needs to be arranged well in advance, as it may be difficult to find someone who can do this.

Always ensure that your dog can be traced should it run away or get lost while on holiday. A little tube with your address, or a tag with home and holiday addresses, can avoid a lot of problems.

Moving home

Dogs generally become more attached to humans than to the house they live in. Moving home is usually not a problem for them. But it can be useful to let the dog get to know its new home and the area around it before moving.

If you can, leave your dog somewhere else (with relatives, friends, or in kennels) on the day of the move. The chance of it running away or getting lost is then practically non-existent. Once you have completed your move, you can pick your dog up and let it quietly get familiar with its new home and environment. Give it its own place in the house at once and it will quickly adapt. At the beginning, always walk your dog on a lead, because an animal can get lost in new surroundings too. Always take a different route so that it gets to know the neighbourhood well.

Don't forget to get your new address and phone number engraved on your dog's tag. Send a change of address notice to the institution that has any chip data. Dogs must sometimes be registered in a new community (just as people), and you will be sent a bill for a dog licence. In some communities, you get part of your fee back if you move within the year you paid for.

A dog is actually more of an omnivore than a carnivore. In the wild it would eat its prey complete with skin and fur, including the bones, stomach, and the innards with their semi-digested vegetable material.

In this way the dog supplements its meat menu with the vitamins and minerals it needs. This is also the basis for feeding a domestic dog.

Ready-made foods

It's not easy for a layman to put together a complete menu for a dog, including all the necessary proteins, fats, vitamins and minerals in just the right proportions and quantities. Meat alone is certainly not a complete meal for a dog, as it contains too little calcium. A continuous calcium deficiency will lead to bone defects, and particularly for a fast-growing puppy this can cause serious skeletal deformities. If you put its food together yourself, you can easily give your dog too much in terms of vitamins and minerals, which can also be bad for your dog's health.

You can avoid these problems by giving your English Springer Spaniel ready-made food of a good brand. These products are well balanced and contain everything your dog needs. Supplements, such as vitamin preparations, are superfluous. The amount of food your dog needs depends on its weight and activity level. You can find guidelines on the packaging.

Split the food into two meals per day if possible, and ensure that there's always a bowl of fresh drinking water next to its food. Give your Springer the time to digest its food and don't let it outdoors straight after a meal. A dog should also never play on a full stomach. This can cause stomach torsion (the stomach turning over), which can be fatal for your dog.

Because the nutritional needs of a dog depend, among other things, on its age and way of life, there are many different types of dog food available. There are puppy foods for young dogs, "light" foods for less active dogs, "energy" foods for working dogs or gundogs and "senior" foods for older dogs.

Puppy food

At present, there is a wide assortment of special (dry) puppy foods available. These chunks contain a higher amount of growth-promoting nutrients, such as protein and calcium. For medium-sized breeds, such as the English Springer Spaniel, these chunks can be dangerous to their health. The dog is already growing fast enough and even faster growth will only promote abnormalities such as Hip and Elbow Dysplasia (see chapter "Your English Springer Spaniel's health"). Therefore feed your Springer puppy only puppy chunks for medium-sized breeds.

Canned foods, mixers and dry foods

Ready-made foods, which are available at pet shops or in the supermarket, can roughly be split into canned food, mixer and dry food. Whichever form you choose, ensure that it's a complete food with all the necessary nutrients. You can see this on the packaging.

Most dogs love canned food. Although the better brands are composed well, they do have one disadvantage: they are soft. A dog fed only on canned food will sooner or later have problems with its teeth (plaque, paradontosis). Besides canned food, give your Springer hard foods or dog chews at certain times.

Mixer is a food consisting of chunks, dried vegetables and grains. Almost all the moisture has been extracted. The advantages of mixer are that it is light and keeps well. You add a certain amount of warm water and the meal is ready. A disadvantage is that it must definitely not be fed without water. Without the extra fluid, mixer will absorb the fluids present in the stomach, which can cause serious problems. Should your dog manage to get at the bag and enjoy its contents, you must immediately give it plenty to drink.
Dry foods also have had moisture extracted, but not as much as

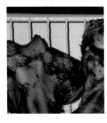

Smoked bones

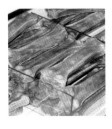

Buffalo hide chews

mixer. The advantage of dry foods is that they are hard, which forces your dog to use its jaws. During chewing, tartar is removed and the gums are massaged.

Dog chew products

Naturally, once in a while you want to spoil your dog with something extra. Don't give it pieces of cheese or sausage as these contain too much salt and fat. There are various products available that a dog will find delicious and which are also healthy, especially for its teeth. You'll find a large range of varying quality in the pet shop.

The butcher's left-overs

The bones of slaughtered animals have traditionally been given to the dog, and dogs are crazy about them, but they are not without risks. Pork and poultry bones are too weak. They can splinter and cause

serious injury to the intestines. Beef bones are more suitable, but they must first be cooked to kill off dangerous bacteria.

Pet shops carry a range of smoked, cooked and dried abattoir residue, such as pigs' ears, bull penis, tripe sticks, oxtails, gullet, dried muscle meat and hoof chews.

Fresh meat

If you do want to give your dog fresh meat occasionally, never give it raw, but always boiled or roasted. Raw (or not fully cooked) pork or chicken can contain life-threatening organisms. Chicken can be contaminated by the notorious salmonella bacteria, while pork can carry the Aujeszky virus. This disease is incurable and will quickly lead to your pet's death.

Cowhide and buffalo hide chews

Dog chews are usually made of buffalo hide or cowhide. The hide is pressed or knotted into chews. Your dog can enjoy chewing on hide in the form of little shoes, twisted sticks, lollies, balls and various other shapes. Nice to look at and a nice change.

Munchie sticks

Munchie sticks are green, yellow, red or brown coloured sticks of various thicknesses. They consist of ground buffalo hide with a number of often undefined additives. Dogs usually love them because these sticks have been dipped in the blood of slaughtered animals. The composition and quality of these between-meal treats is not always clear. Some are fine, but there have also been sticks found that contained high levels of cardboard and even paint residues. Choose a product whose ingredients are clearly labelled.

Overweight?

Recent investigations have shown that many dogs are overweight. A dog usually becomes too fat because of over-feeding and lack of exercise. Use of medicines or a disease is rarely the cause.

Dogs that become too fat are often given too much food or too many treats between meals. Gluttony or boredom can also be a cause, and a dog often puts on weight following castration or sterilisation. Due to changes in hormone levels it becomes less active and consumes less energy. Finally, simply too little exercise alone can lead to a dog becoming overweight. In the case of the English Springer Spaniel in particular, too little exercise is often the cause of the dog becoming overweight. Springers are very active dogs that need to have exercise for several hours a day. You can use the following rule of thumb to check whether your dog is overweight: you should be able to feel its ribs, but not see them. If you can't feel its ribs then your

dog is much too fat. Overweight dogs live a passive life; they play and run too little and tire quickly. They also suffer from all kinds of medical problems (problems in joints and heart conditions). They usually die younger too.

So it's important to make sure that your dog doesn't become too fat. Always follow the guidelines on food packaging. Adapt them if your dog is less active or gets lots of snacks. Try to ensure that your dog gets plenty of exercise by playing and running with it as much as you can. If your dog starts to show signs of putting on weight, you can switch to a low-calorie food. If it's really too fat and reducing its food quantity doesn't help, then a special diet is the only solution.

Munchie sticks

Caring for your English Springer Spaniel

Good (daily) care is very important for your dog's well-being.

A well cared-for dog is at less risk of becoming ill. Caring for your dog is not just a necessity, but also a pleasure: dog and owner are giving each other all their attention for a moment. It is also a good opportunity for a game and a cuddle.

The coat

Taking care of your dog's coat consists of regularly brushing or combing it and checking it for parasites (such as fleas). How often a dog needs to be brushed or combed depends on the length of the coat. Use the right equipment for taking care of your dog's coat. Combs must not be too sharp. Choose a brush made

of rubber or natural hair and also buy a pair of effilating scissors. Always brush or comb your dog from head to tail, following the direction the hair lies in. If you get your puppy used to having its coat cared for at an early age, it will learn to enjoy its grooming sessions.

An English Springer Spaniel needs to be groomed every day. With a soft brush, remove all loose hairs from the coat on the back. The feathering (i.e. the long hair on the ears, legs and the body) needs to be combed with a coarse comb. Make sure that you thoroughly brush the armpits and behind the ears, as the hair tangles up easily here. Another reason why it is important to take care of your dog's coat is to prevent unpleasant odours developing from the dead hair.

The hair between the foot pads needs to be cut back regularly. You normally need to do it every eight weeks. Also check the length of the feathering on the tail. If it becomes too long it will make the tail too heavy. This badly affects the way your dog carries its tail. Feathering that is too long can be cut with special effilating scissors (thinning scissors). A normal pair of scissors won't do here.

The hair on the inside of the ear also needs to be removed around the auditory duct. Use a pair of effilating scissors for this too. Removing this hair will let fresh air get to the ears and thus helps to prevent ear problems.

Trimming

Your English Springer Spaniel needs a good trimming session three to four times a year. The hair at the feet and around the auditory duct needs to be trimmed more often. When trimming your English Springer, you need to pluck all dead hair out of its coat and thus thin it out. If you intend to take your dog to shows, let a professional dog groomer do the trimming. You can have your dog trimmed at a professional dog grooming parlour and sometimes even at the breeder's. Tell the groomer beforehand whether you want a show trim or not. The breed association also supplies information on how to care for

your Springer's coat. 'Trimming demonstrations' are often held at events, so that you can learn the art of trimming.

Bathing your dog

Only bathe your English Springer Spaniel when it is absolutely necessary, and always use a special dog shampoo when doing so. Make sure that no shampoo can get into your dog's ears and eyes, and always rinse the suds out well. Only let your dog outdoors when it is completely dry, as dogs can catch colds too! Your vet can prescribe certain medicinal shampoos for different skin conditions. Always follow the instructions. Good flea control is very important to prevent skin and coat disorders. You need to fight fleas not only on the dog itself, but

teeth regularly. If you think that all is not well, contact your vet. Regular feeds of hard dry feed help to keep your dog's teeth clean and healthy. There are special dog chews that help to prevent build-up of tartar and to keep the breath fresh.

The best way to keep your dog's teeth healthy is by brushing them regularly. You can use a special toothbrush for dogs for this, but a piece of gauze wrapped round a finger will also do the job. If you get your dog used to having its teeth cleaned at a young age, you won't have any problems later. You can also get an older dog used to having its teeth cared for. With a dog treat as a reward, it certainly won't mind.

Nails

On dogs that regularly walk on hard surfaces the nails will grind themselves down to the right length. It is not necessary to clip them in this case. It won't do any harm, however, to check the length of the nails at certain times, especially on dogs that don't go out on the streets a lot. With the help of a piece of paper, you can easily see if your dog's nails are too long. If you can push the paper between the ground and the nail of the (standing) dog, the nail has the right length. Also remember to regularly check the length of the fifth nail on the front paws.

also in its environment (see chapter "Parasites"). Coat problems can also be the result of allergies to certain feed components. In this case, the vet can prescribe a hypoallergenic diet.

Teeth

Your Springer needs to be able to eat properly to stay in good condition. It thus needs healthy teeth. Therefore check your dog's

Nails that are too long can bother a dog. It can injure itself when scratching. They thus need to be cut. You can do this with special scissors, which you can buy in pet shops. Be careful not to cut the nail too far back, as you could cut into the quick. This can bleed profusely. If you feel unsure about cutting your dog's nails, let the vet or a grooming parlour do this necessary task.

Eyes

You need to clean your dog's eyes every day, as 'sleepies' and bits of dried tear fluid can collect in the corners of the eyes. You can easily remove these by wiping downwards with your thumb. If you do not like doing this, you can use a bit of toilet paper or a tissue.

Cleaning your dog's eyes only takes a few seconds a day, so don't miss it! If the sleepies become yellow and slimy, it is usually a sign of a serious irritation or an infection. Eye drops (available from your vet's) usually solve this problem quite quickly.

Ears

The ears are often forgotten when looking after dogs. They need to be checked at least once a week, however, especially on dogs with hanging ears, such as the English Springer Spaniel. Due to the shape of the ears and the hair that grows around the ear canal, air gets to them insufficiently. This can cause ear problems.

As the hair in the Springer's ears can cause problems, it is best to remove it. Carefully pluck the hairs out between your thumbs and index fingers. If the auricle is very dirty or contains too much wax, you need to clean it. Preferably use a clean cotton cloth moistened with some warm water or baby oil for this. It is inadvisable to use cotton wool due to the fluff it can leave behind. Never enter the ear canal with an object! If you neglect cleaning your dog's ears, there's a risk of ear infection. A dog that scratches its ears a lot might be suffering from dirty ears, an ear infection or ear mites. A visit to the vet's will be inevitable.

Bringing up your English Springer Spaniel

It is very important that your English Springer Spaniel is well brought up and that it listens to you. This will make it not only more pleasant for you, but also for your environment. A puppy can learn what it may and may not do in a playful manner.

(Dis)obedience

Rewarding and consistency are very important aids when bringing up your dog. If you always reward it for good behaviour with your voice, a pat or a treat, it will quickly learn to obey. A puppy course can help you along the way.

A dog that won't obey you is not just a problem for you, but also for your surroundings. It's therefore important to avoid unwanted behaviour. In fact, this is what training your dog is all about, so get started early. 'Start 'em young!' should be your motto.

An untrained dog is not just a nuisance, but can also cause dangerous situations by running into the road, chasing joggers or jumping at people. A dog must be trained out of this undesirable behaviour as quickly as possible. The longer you let it go on, the more difficult it will become to correct. The best thing to do is to attend a special obedience course. This won't only help to correct the dog's behaviour, but its owner also learns how to handle undesirable behaviour at home. A dog must not only obey its master during training, but at home too.

Always be consistent when training good behaviour and correcting annoying behaviour. This means your dog may always behave in a certain way, or must never behave that way. Always reward your dog for good behaviour and never punish it after the event for any wrongdoing. If your dog finally comes after you've been calling it a long time, then reward it. If you're angry because you had to wait so long, it may feel it's actually being punished for coming. It will probably not obey at all next time for fear of punishment.

Try to take no notice of undesirable behaviour. Your dog will perceive your reaction (even a negative one) as a reward for this behaviour. If you need to correct your dog, then do this immediately. Use your voice or grip it by the scruff of its neck and push it to the ground. This is the way a bitch calls her pups to order. Rewards for good behaviour are, by far, preferable to punishment; they always achieve a better result.

House-training

The very first training (and one of the most important) that a dog needs is house-training. The basis for good house-training is keeping a close eye on your puppy. If you pay attention, you will notice that it will sniff around a long time and turn around a certain spot before doing its business there. Pick it up gently and place it outdoors, always at the same place. Reward it abundantly if it does its business there.

Another good moment for house-training is after eating or sleeping. A puppy often needs to do its business at these times. Let it relieve itself before playing with it, otherwise it will forget to do so and you'll not reach your goal. For the first few days, take your puppy out for a walk just after it's eaten or woken up. It will quickly understand your intention, especially if it's rewarded with a dog biscuit for a successful attempt.

Of course, it's not always possible to go out after every snack or snooze. Lay newspapers at different spots in the house. Whenever the pup needs to do its business, place it on a newspaper. After some time it will start to look for a place itself. Then start to reduce the number of newspapers. Finally, there will be just one newspaper left, at the front or back door. The puppy will learn to go to the door if it needs to relieve itself. Then you put it on the lead and go out with it. You can eventually remove the last newspaper. Your puppy is now house-trained.

One thing that certainly won't work is punishing an accident after the event. A dog whose nose is rubbed in its urine or its droppings won't understand that at all. It will only get frightened of you. Rewarding works much better than punishment. An indoor kennel or cage can be a good tool to help in house-training. A puppy won't foul its own nest, so a kennel can be a good solution for the night, or during periods in the day when you can't watch it. But a kennel must not become a prison where your puppy is locked up day and night.

First exercises

The basic commands for an obedient dog are those for sit, lie down, come and stay. You can teach a pup to sit by holding a piece of dog biscuit above its nose and then slowly moving it backwards. The puppy's head will also move backwards until its hind legs slowly go down. At that moment you call 'Sit!'. After a few attempts, it will quickly get the idea of this nice game. Use the 'Sit!' command before you give your dog its food, put it on the lead, or before it's allowed to cross the street.

Teaching the command to lie down is similar. Instead of moving the piece of dog biscuit backwards, move it down vertically until your hand reaches the ground and then forwards.

The dog will also move its forepaws forwards and lie down on its own. At that moment call 'Lie down!' or 'Lay!'. This command is useful when you want your dog to be quiet.

Two people are needed for the 'Come!' command. One holds the dog back while the other runs away. After a few metres he stops and enthusiastically calls 'Come!'. The other person now lets the dog go, and it should obey the command at once. Again you reward it abundantly. Slowly increase the distance between yourself and your dog. The 'Come!' command is useful in many situations and good for safety too.

A dog learns to stay from the sitting or lying position. While it's sitting or lying down, you call the command 'Stay!' and then step back one step. If the dog moves with you, quietly put it back in position, without displaying anger. If you do react angrily, you're actually punishing it for coming to you, and you'll only confuse your dog. It can't understand that coming is rewarded one time, and punished another. Once the dog stays nicely, reward it abundantly. At the beginning, you can ask a helper to hold the dog (on the lead). Practise this exercise while increasing the distances between your dog and yourself (at first no more than one metre/ 3 ft). The

'Stay!' command is useful when getting out of the car.

Obedience courses
Obedience courses to help you bring up your dog are available throughout the UK. These courses do not just teach owner and dog a lot, but are also fun.

With a puppy, you can begin with a puppy course. This is designed to provide the basic training. A puppy that has attended such a course has learned about all kinds of things that will confront it in later life: other dogs, humans, traffic and more. The puppy will also learn obedience and to follow a number of basic commands. Apart from all that, attention will be given to important subjects such as grooming, being alone, travelling in a car, and doing its business in the right places.

The next step after a puppy course is a course for young dogs. This course repeats the basic exercises and ensures that the growing dog doesn't get into bad habits. After this, the dog can move on to an obedience course for fully grown dogs.

For more information on where to find courses in your area, contact your local kennel club. You can get its address from the Kennel Club of Great Britain in London. In some areas, the RSPCA organises obedience classes and your local

branch may be able to give you information.

Play and toys

There are various ways to play with your Springer. You can romp and run with it, but also play a number of games, such as retrieving, tug-of-war, hide-and-seek and catch. A tennis ball is ideal for retrieving, and you can play tug-of-war with an old sock or a special tugging rope. Start with tug-of-war only when your dog is a year old. A puppy must first get its second teeth and then they need several months to strengthen. There's a real chance of your dog's teeth becoming deformed if it starts playing tug-of-war too soon. You can use almost anything for a game of hide-and-seek. Frisbees are ideal for catching games. Never use too small a ball for games, as it can easily get lodged into the dog's throat.

Play is extremely important. Not only does it strengthen the bond between dog and master, but it's also healthy for both. Make sure that you're always the one that ends the game. Only stop when the dog has brought back the ball or frisbee, and make sure that you always win the tug-of-war. This confirms your dominant position in the hierarchy. Use these toys only during play, so that your dog doesn't forget their significance.

When choosing a special dog toy, remember that dogs are hardly careful with them. So always buy toys of good quality, which your dog can't easily destroy. Be also very careful with sticks and twigs. The latter, particularly, can easily splinter. A splinter of wood in your dog's throat or intestines can cause awful problems. Throwing sticks or twigs can also be dangerous. If they stick into the

ground, a dog can easily run into them with its mouth open.

If you want to do more than just playing the odd game with your dog, you can do lots of different types of dog sports. If you are looking for a challenge, have a look at activities such as flyball, agility, doggydancing, dogfrisbee and obedience certificates. You can also join a hunting club.

Aggression

English Springer Spaniels are normally never aggressive. It can, however, happen that even your Springer is less friendly towards other animals or people. It is therefore good to have some background information about canine aggression. There are two different main types of aggressive behaviour in dogs: The anxious-aggressive dog and the dominant-aggressive dog.

An anxious-aggressive dog can be recognised by its pulled-back ears and its lowly held tail. It will have pulled in its lips, baring its teeth. This dog is aggressive because it's very frightened and feels cornered. It would prefer to run away, but if it can't then it will bite to defend itself. It will grab its victim anywhere it can. The attack is usually brief and as soon as the dog can see a way to escape it's gone. In a confrontation with other dogs, it will normally turn out as the loser. It can become more

aggressive once it's realised that people or other animals are afraid of it. You can't change this behaviour just like that. You first have to try to understand what the dog is afraid of. Getting professional help is a good idea here, as the wrong approach can easily make the problem worse.

The dominant-aggressive dog's body language is very different. Its ears are pricked and its tail is raised and stiff. This dog will only go for its victim's arms, legs or throat. It is self-assured and highly placed in the dog hierarchy. Its attack is a display of power rather than a consequence of fear. This dog needs to know who's the

boss. You must bring it up rigorously and with a strong hand. An obedience course can help.

A dog may also show aggression when in pain. This is a natural defensive reaction. In this case try to resolve your dog's fear as far as possible. Reward it for letting you get to the painful spot. Be careful, because a frightened dog in pain may also bite its master! Muzzling it can help prevent problems if you have to do something that may be painful. Never punish a dog for this type of aggression!

Fear

English Springer Spaniels are not anxious dogs by nature. If your dog displays overly anxious behaviour, the cause can usually be found in the first few weeks of its life. A lack of new experiences in this very important so-called 'socialisation phase' has a big influence on the adult dog's behaviour. If a dog does not get to see humans, other dogs or other animals during this phase, it will be afraid of them later. This is common with dogs that have grown up in a barn or kennel with basically no human contact. As mentioned earlier, fear can lead to aggression. It is thus very important that your dog gets as many new experiences as possible during its first few weeks. Take it into town in the car or on the bus, walk down a busy street with it and let it have lots of contact with people, other dogs and other animals/ pets.

It's a huge task to turn an anxious, poorly socialised dog into a real pet. It will probably take an enormous amount of attention, love, patience and energy to get such an animal used to everything around it. Reward it often and give it plenty of time to adapt and, over time, it will learn to trust you and become less anxious. Try not to force anything, because that will always have the reverse effect. Here too, an obedience course can help a lot.

A dog can be especially afraid of strangers. Have visitors give it something tasty as a treat when they arrive. Put a can of dog biscuits by the door, so that your visitors can spoil your dog when they come in the door. Once again, don't try to force anything. If your dog is still frightened, it is best to leave it in peace.

Dogs are often frightened in certain situations; well known examples are thunderstorms and fireworks. In these cases try to ignore your dog's anxious behaviour. If you react to its whimpering and whining, it's the same as rewarding it. If you ignore its fear completely, your dog will quickly learn that nothing is wrong. You can speed up this 'learning process' by rewarding its positive behaviour.

Rewarding

Rewarding forms the basis for bringing up a dog. Rewarding good behaviour works far better than punishing bad behaviour and rewarding is also much more fun. Over time the opinions on how to bring up dogs have gradually changed. In the past, a sharp pull on the lead was considered the appropriate way to correct bad behaviour. Today, experts view rewards as a positive incentive to get dogs to do what we expect of them.

There are many ways of rewarding your dog. The usual ways are a pat or a friendly word, even without a tasty treat to go with it. When bringing up a puppy, a tasty treat at the right moment will do wonders, though. Make sure that you always have something tasty in your pocket to reward it for good behaviour.

Another form of reward is play. Dogs love to play. Whenever a dog notices that you have a ball in your pocket, it won't go far from your side. As soon as you've finished playing, put the ball away. This way your dog will always do its best in exchange for a game. Despite the emphasis you put on rewarding good behaviour, a dog can sometimes be a nuisance or disobedient. You must correct such behaviour immediately. Always be consistent: once 'no' must always be 'no'.

Barking

Dogs that bark too much and too often are a nuisance for their surroundings. A dog-owner may tolerate barking up to a point, but neighbours are often annoyed by the unnecessary noise. Luckily, English Springer Spaniels do not bark excessively by nature. Don't encourage your puppy to bark and yelp. Of course, it should be able to announce its presence, but if it goes on barking it must be called to order with a strict 'Quiet!'. If the puppy does not obey, you can hold its muzzle closed with your hand for a moment.

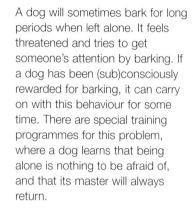

A dog will sometimes bark for long periods when left alone. It feels threatened and tries to get someone's attention by barking. If a dog has been (sub)consciously rewarded for barking, it can carry on with this behaviour for some time. There are special training programmes for this problem, where a dog learns that being alone is nothing to be afraid of, and that its master will always return.

This is how you can practise with your dog: Leave the room and come back in at once. Reward your dog if it stays quiet. Gradually increase the length of your absences and keep rewarding it as long as it remains quiet. Never punish your dog if it does bark or yelp. It will never understand punishment afterwards, and this will only make the problem worse. Never go back into the room as long as your dog displays the unwanted behaviour, as it will view this as a reward.

You might want to make your dog feel more comfortable by switching the radio on for company during your absence. It will eventually learn that you always come back and the barking will reduce. If you don't get the required result, attend an obedience course with your dog.

It is very important that your English Springer Spaniel is well brought up and that it listens to you. This will make it not only more pleasant for you, but also for your environment. A puppy can learn what it may and may not do in a playful manner.

Those who simply want a 'cosy companion' however, will miss the regular adventures with females on heat and unrestrainable males like a hole in the head. But knowing a little about canine reproduction will help you to understand why they behave the way they do, and what measures you need to take when this happens.

Liability

Breeding dogs is much more than simply 1+1= many. If you're planning to breed with your English Springer Spaniel, be on your guard. The whole affair can quite easily turn into a financial disaster, because, under the law, a breeder is liable for the 'quality' of his puppies.

The breed association places high demands on animals used for breeding. They need to be checked for possible (hereditary) abnormalities (see chapter "Your English Springer Spaniel's health"). By adhering to these rules, a breeder shows that he cares. If you breed a litter and sell the puppies without these tests having been made, you can be held liable by the new owners for any possible costs resulting from any hereditary abnormality! And these (vet's) bills can be very expensive! It is therefore advisable to contact a breeding association, if you're thinking about breeding a litter of English Springer Spaniels.

The female in season

Bitches become sexually mature at the age of eight to twelve months. This is when they come into season for the first time. A normal season lasts two to three weeks. During this time, the bitch loses drops of blood and is very appealing to males. The bitch is fertile during the second half of her season, and she will then accept dogs to mate. The best time for mating is between the ninth and thirteenth day of her season.

A female's first season is often shorter and less severe than those that follow. If you do want to breed with your bitch, you must allow the first (and sometimes the second) season to pass. Most bitches go into season twice per year.

If you do plan to breed with your English Springer Spaniel bitch in the future, then sterilisation is not an option to prevent unwanted offspring. A temporary solution is a contraceptive injection, although this is controversial because of possible side effects such as uterus infections.

Phantom pregnancy

A phantom pregnancy is a not uncommon occurrence with

dogs. The female behaves as if she has a litter. She takes all kinds of things to her basket and treats them like puppies. Her milk teats swell up and sometimes milk is actually produced. The female will sometimes behave aggressively towards people or other animals, as if she is defending her young.

Phantom pregnancies usually begin two months after a season and can last a number of weeks. If it happens to a bitch once, it will often re-occur after every season. If she suffers badly from it, sterilisation is the best solution, because constantly re-occurring phantom pregnancies increase the risk of womb or teat conditions.

In the short term a hormone treatment is worth trying, perhaps also homeopathic medicines. Camphor spirit can give relief when teats are heavily swollen, but rubbing the teats with ice or a cold cloth (moisten and freeze) can also help to relieve the pain. Feed the female less than usual, and make sure she gets enough distraction and extra exercise.

Preparing to breed

If you do plan to breed a litter of puppies, you must first wait for your female to be physically and mentally fully grown before you have her covered. In any event you must wait until her second

season. To mate a bitch, you need a male. You could simply let her out on the street and she would quickly return home pregnant. If you want to breed purebred English Springers, it would, of course, be unwise to have your bitch covered by the next-best candidate, even if she does not have a pedigree. You should therefore be meticulous with your preparations. Think especially about the following: Accompanying a bitch through pregnancy, birth and the first eight to twelve weeks afterwards is a time-consuming affair.

Never breed with English Springer Spaniels that have congenital defects, and this also applies to dogs without papers. The same goes for hyperactive, nervous and shy dogs. If your Springer has a pedigree, then have her covered by a dog that also has one. Contact a breed association for more information on this topic.

Pregnancy

It's often difficult to tell at first if a bitch is pregnant. Only after about four weeks can you feel the pups in her belly. She will now slowly become fatter and her behaviour will usually change. Her teats will swell up during the last few weeks of pregnancy.

The average pregnancy lasts 63 days and costs the bitch a lot of energy. In the beginning she is fed her normal amount of food, but her nutritional needs increase in jumps during the second half of the pregnancy. Give her approximately fifteen percent more food each week from the fifth week on. The mother-to-be needs extra energy and proteins during this phase of her pregnancy. During the last weeks you can give her a concentrated food that is rich in energy, such as dry puppy food. Divide this into several small portions per day, as she can no longer deal with large portions of food. Towards the end of the pregnancy, her energy needs can easily be one-and-a-half times more than usual. After about seven weeks the mother will start to demonstrate

nesting behaviour and to look for a place to give birth to her young. This might be her own basket or a special birthing box. This must be ready at least a week before the birth to give the mother-to-be time to get used to it. The basket or box should preferably be in a quiet place.

The birth
On average, three to nine puppies are born in a litter. The birth normally passes without problems. If you are in any doubt, you need to contact your vet immediately, of course!

Suckling and weaning
After giving birth, the mother starts to produce milk. The suckling period is very demanding. During the first three to four weeks the pups rely entirely on their mother's milk. During this time she needs extra food and fluids. This can be up to three to four times the normal amount. If she's producing too little milk, you can give both the mother and her young special puppy milk.

Here too, divide the high quantity of food the mother needs into several smaller portions. Again, choose a concentrated high-energy food and give her plenty of fresh drinking water. Do not give the bitch cow's milk, as this can cause diarrhoea.

You can give the puppies some supplemental solid food when they are three to four weeks old. There are special puppy foods available

that follow on well from the mother's milk and can easily be eaten with the puppies' milk teeth.

Ideally, the puppies are fully weaned at an age of six to seven weeks, i.e. they no longer drink their mother's milk. The mother's milk production gradually stops and her food needs also drop. Within a few weeks after weaning, the mother should be back to getting the same amount of food as before the pregnancy.

Castration and sterilisation

As soon as you are sure that your bitch should never bear a (new) litter, a vasectomy or sterilisation is the best solution. During sterilisation (in fact this is normal castration) the ovaries and often the uterus are removed surgically. The bitch no longer goes into season and can no longer become pregnant. The best age for a sterilisation is about eighteen months, when the bitch is more or less fully grown.

A male dog is usually only castrated for medical reasons or to correct undesirable sexual behaviour. During a castration the testicles are removed, which is a simple procedure and usually without complications. There is no special age for castration but, where possible, wait until the dog is fully grown. Vasectomy is sufficient where it's only a case of making the dog infertile. In this case the dog keeps its sexual drive but can no longer reproduce.

As mentioned earlier, English Springer Spaniels are dogs that enjoy living a very active life. They are particularly keen on doing things with their master.

If you regularly participate in activities with your English Springer Spaniel, you will notice not only that the bond between both of you is becoming stronger, but also that your dog is much calmer in the house and a lot more obedient. In this chapter you will find a brief overview over different activities. Contact the breed association if you want more information on this matter.

Gundog training
Hunting clubs organise gundog training for all gundog breeds every year. Some trainers specialise in training only English Springer Spaniels. Most breed association also have special gundog trials commissions. Most breed associations also include in their goals to further the training of English Springer Spaniels in general and in hunt training in particular. To be able to participate in gundog training, your English Springer Spaniel will often be required to hold obedience certificates and sometimes even to have attended a basic course.

Behaviour and obedience
You can choose from a variety of obedience training courses, starting with those for puppies. English Springer Spaniels generally really enjoy this type of training: their strong will to please makes them want to execute the exercises as well as possible. After

the basic obedience training course, you can carry on training for a number of obedience certificates.

Retrieving

The sport of retrieving is very closely linked to hunting. The most important difference is that the retrieving sport is open to all dog breeds (and thus also to non-gundog breeds) and that training is not with real game. Both bumpers and wooden and synthetic training dummies are used. The tests are set in such a way that they can be practised on the grounds of dog schools. There are different ways that you can enjoy retrieving as a sport, such as working trials and as part of gundog training.

Agility

In this sport, the dog has to master a certain course accompanied by its owner. Different types of obstacles need to be overcome on the way. The task is to complete the course as quickly as possible and with as few mistakes as possible. Agility competitions are often organised by local kennel clubs. The English

Sports and shows

Springer Spaniel is a fast, intelligent dog that will really enjoy this type of dog sport.

Flyball
Flyball is another type of dog sport. A flyball team consists of dog owners, their dogs, a coach and a person loading the balls into the apparatus. The number of participants can vary from five to eight dog/owner combinations. First the dog has to jump over four small fences, and then it has to push down a plank on the flyball apparatus with its paw. This action 'launches' a ball, which the dog needs to catch. The dog has to jump over the fences again on its way back and carry the ball to its owner as quickly as possible. The dog with the fastest time wins here too.

Endurance trials
Dogs that have learned to run next to the bike will normally really enjoy this. It is also very good for their muscular development, as the body moves in a nice and regular manner. This strengthens the muscles without over-burdening the joints. Do not let your English Springer Spaniel run next to the bike before it is at least a year old. Starting too early is bad for the development of the bones. Slowly increase the distance. Do not let your dog run next to the bike when it is too warm, do not feed it just before taking it out and don't go for too long. Advanced English Springers can participate in endurance competitions. The dog will need to cover a distance of twenty kilometres (12 miles) next to the bike with an average speed of fifteen to twenty kilometres (9 to 12 miles) per hour.

Dog shows
Visiting a dog show is a pleasant experience for both dog and master, and for some dog-lovers it has become an intensive hobby. They visit countless shows every year. Others find it nice to visit an exemption show with their dog just once. It's worth making the effort to visit an exemption show where a judge's experienced eyes

will inspect your English Springer Spaniel and assess it for build, gaits, condition and behaviour. The judge's report will tell you your dog's weak and strong points. This can be very useful when choosing a mate for breeding, for example. You can also exchange experiences with other English Springer owners. Official dog shows are only open to dogs with pedigrees.

Ring training

If you've never been to an exemption show, you're probably tapping in the dark in terms of what will be expected of you and your dog. Many kennel clubs organise so-called ring training courses for dogs going to an exemption show for the first time. This training teaches you exactly what the judge will be looking for, and you can practise the correct techniques together with your dog. You will also be informed on how your English Springer Spaniel should be trimmed to look the part.

Club matches

Almost all kennel clubs and breed associations organise club matches. You have to enter your dog in a certain class before the big day. These meetings are usually small and friendly and are often the first acquaintance dog and master make with a real judge. This is an overwhelming experience for your dog - a lot of

its contemporaries and a strange man or woman who fiddles around with it and peers into its mouth. Of course you will have had the opportunity to prepare for this during ring training. After a few times, your dog will know exactly what's expected of it and will happily go to the next club match.

Championship shows

Various championship shows take place during the course of the year, all of which offer different prizes. These shows are much more strictly organised than club matches. Here, too, your dog must be registered in a certain class in advance and it will then be listed in a catalogue. On the day itself, the dog is kept in a cage (indoor kennel) until its turn comes up. During the judging in the ring, it's important that you show your dog at its best. The judge will give an official verdict

Sports and shows

and write a report. When all the dogs from that class have been judged, the winner is selected. You can pick up your report, and possibly your prize, after the class has finished.

The winners of the various classes will then compete for the title of "Best of Breed". A winner will be chosen from the dogs belonging to the same breed group. The various winners of the different breed groups will then compete for "Best in Show".

It goes without saying that your dog has to be in top condition for a show. The judge will not be pleased if your dog's coat is dirty or tangled up and if its paws are covered in mud. Its nails must be clipped and its teeth free of tartar. Your dog must also be free of any parasites or illnesses. A bitch must not be in season, and a dog should have both its testicles. Judges also don't like badly brought up, frightened or nervous dogs. If you want to know more about shows, contact your local kennel club or the breed association.

Do not forget!
If you want to visit a show with your English Springer Spaniel, you need to be well prepared. You must certainly not forget the following:

For yourself
• Registration card
• Food and drink
• Safety pin for the catalogue number
• Chair(s)

For your dog
• Food and drink bowls and food
• Dog blanket and perhaps a cushion
• Show lead
• Grooming equipment
• Vaccination book and other papers for your dog

All dogs are vulnerable to various sorts of parasites. Parasites are tiny creatures that live at the expense of another animal. They feed on blood, skin and other body substances.

There are two main types. Internal parasites live within their host animal's body (tapeworm and roundworm) and external parasites live on the animal's exterior, usually in its coat (fleas and ticks), but also in its ears (ear mite).

Fleas

Fleas feed on a dog's blood. They cause not only itching and skin problems, but can also carry infections such as tapeworm. In large numbers they can even cause anaemia and dogs can also become allergic to a flea's saliva, which can cause serious skin conditions.

So it's important that you treat your dog for fleas as effectively as possible. Do not just treat the animal itself, but also its surroundings. There are various medicines for treating your dog: drops for the neck and to put in its food, flea collars, long-life sprays and flea powders. There are various sprays in pet shops, which can be used to eradicate fleas in your dog's immediate surroundings. Choose a spray that kills both adult fleas and their larvae. If your dog goes in your car, you should spray that too.

Fleas can also affect other pets, so you should treat those too. When spraying a room, cover any aquarium or fishbowl present. If the spray reaches the water, it can be fatal for your fish!

Your vet and pet shop have a wide range of flea treatments and can offer you more detailed advice on this subject.

Ticks

Ticks are small, spider-like parasites. They feed on the blood of the animal or person they've settled on. A tick looks like a tiny, grey-coloured leather bag with eight feet. When it has sucked itself full, it is darker in colour and can easily be five to ten times its own size.

Dogs usually fall victim to ticks in bushes, woods or long grass. Ticks cause not only irritation by their blood-sucking, but can also carry a number of serious diseases. This applies especially to the Mediterranean countries, which can be infested with blood parasites. In our country these diseases are fortunately less common. But Lyme disease, which can also affect humans, has reached our shores. Your vet can prescribe a special treatment if you're planning to take your dog to southern Europe. It is important to fight ticks as effectively as possible. Check your dog regularly, especially when it's been running free in woods and bushes. It can also wear an anti-tick collar.

Removing a tick is simple using tick tweezers. Grip the tick with the tweezers, as close to the dog's skin as possible, and carefully pull it out. You can also grip the tick between your fingers and, turning it, carefully pull it out. You must disinfect the spot where the tick was, using iodine to prevent infection. Never soak the tick in alcohol, ether or oil. In a shock reaction the tick may discharge the infected contents of its stomach into the dog's skin.

Tick

Worms

Dogs can suffer from various types of worm. The most common are tapeworm and roundworm. Tapeworm causes diarrhoea and poor condition. With a tapeworm infection you can sometimes find small pieces of the worm around the dog's anus or on its bed. In this case, the dog must be wormed immediately. You should also check your dog for fleas, as these can carry the tapeworm infection.

Roundworm is another condition that reoccurs regularly. Puppies are often infected by their mother's milk. Roundworm causes problems (particularly in younger dogs), such as diarrhoea, loss of weight and stagnated growth. In serious cases the pup becomes thin, but with a swollen belly. It may vomit and you can then see the worms in its vomit. They are spaghetti-like tendrils. In its first year, a puppy needs to be treated with a worm treatment regularly. Adult dogs should be treated at least twice a year.

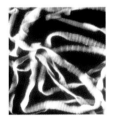

Tapeworms

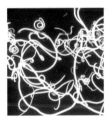

Roundworms

We will provide you with some brief information on illnesses and abnormalities that are more commonly found with the English Springer than with any other breed.

Hip Dysplasia (HD)

Hip Dysplasia is an abnormality of the hip joints, whereby the socket of the hip joint fails to enclose the head of the upper thigh properly. This causes inflammation and bone tumours, which can be very painful. Until recently, it was assumed that HD was primarily caused by genetic factors. Recent investigations, however, indicate that, while genetic factors certainly play a role in terms of the susceptibility to HD, external factors such as food quality and exercise appear at least as important.

Limit the chance of HD as far as possible by giving your dog ready-made food of a good brand, and don't add any supplements! Make sure your dog doesn't become too fat. An English Springer Spaniel puppy must be watched closely during its first year. Don't let it romp too much with other dogs or chase sticks and balls too wildly. These kinds of games cause the pup to make abrupt and risky movements, which can overburden its soft joints. One important but underestimated factor behind HD is the floor in your home. Parquet and tiled floors are much too slippery for a young dog. Regular slipping can cause complications that promote HD. If you have a smooth floor, it's advisable to lay blankets or old carpet in places the dog uses regularly. Let it spend lots of time in the garden, as grass is a perfect surface to run to.

Luckily there are not many English Springer Spaniels suffering from HD. The breed associations try tries to keep it that way by strictly testing potential breeding animals. An examination for HD is therefore mandatory for any animals intended for breeding.

The current scoring scheme of the BVA/KC for hip dysplasia (HD) is operational since 1984; it tells us the following:

"The hip score is the sum of the points awarded for each of nine aspects of the X-rays of both hip joints. The minimum hip score is 0 and the maximum is 106 (53 for each hip). The lower the score the

less the degree of hip dysplasia present. An average (or mean) score is calculated for all breeds scored under the scheme and advice for breeders is to use only breeding stock with scores well below the breed mean score." More information is available at: www.bva.co.uk.

Elbow Dysplasia (ED)

Elbow Dysplasia generally appears during the first year of a puppy's life. This condition is similar to HD, but affects the forelegs. In the worst case ED can cause lameness. An operation is then needed, which is usually successful. The measures you can take to reduce the chance of ED are the same as for HD.

Progressive Retina Atrophy (PRA)

Progressive Retina Atrophy (PRA) is a degeneration of the retina that inevitably leads to blindness. In the beginning phase, i.e. until it is approximately five years old, the dog will still be able to see well during the day. It will become totally blind at an age of between five to nine years.

Cataracts

The examination for Cataracts is conducted at the same time as the tests for PRA.

Cataracts causes a clouding of the retina and gives a blurry vision. It can occur at a young age.

Entropion and Ectropion

These are hereditary abnormalities of the eyelids. In the case of Entropion the eyelids curl inwards, in the case of Ectropion they curl outwards. Because the eyelashes come to lie on the eyeball, an irritation is caused that leads to red watering eyes. The eyes can become infected and pussy. This can eventually lead to damage to the cornea and even to blindness. Entropion and Ectropion can be corrected surgically.

Retina Dysplasia (RD)

Retina Dysplasia (RD) is an eye condition that is already present before birth. With RD the two layers of the eye's retina are not properly attached to each other. Retina Dysplasia is not progressive and thus does not become worse. Puppies can be checked for RD from an age of six to eight weeks. Their small eyes and the fact that they find it difficult to sit still at this age sometimes make another examination at the age of

approximately six months necessary. In most dog breeds RD is caused by genetic factors, but in exceptional cases it can be caused prenatal by a Herpes or a Parvo infection.

If you buy a puppy via the breed association, both parent animals should have been certified as free of hereditary eye abnormalities. Both parent animals should be free of PRA, Cataracts and RD.

Ear infection

Ear infections are quite common with dogs, especially in breeds with hanging ears. The animal shakes its head and scratches its ears a lot and it might even whine with pain. The external auditory duct is usually dirty and red, but the ear itself (internal auditory duct) is usually also dirty, red and warm, and gives off an unpleasant smell.
Ear infections can be caused by infestation with ear mites or an infection of the auditory duct with bacteria and/or fungi. Let a vet examine the infected ear. He can prescribe an ointment and maybe medication that will suppress the itching. It is important that plenty of air can get to the ear, so remove excessive hair from the auditory duct on a regular basis.

The risk associated with the scratching and shaking is an aural haematoma. A huge swelling of the auricle develops, which requires surgery or at least treatment. If it is not treated in the right way, a very painful "cauliflower ear" will develop.

The year 1902 was historic for the English Springer Spaniel: The Kennel Club recognized the breed as a specific spaniel variety and gave it a separate breed classification.

Between 1902 to 1912 the English Springer Spaniel grew in popularity. The breed did well both as a shooting dog and as a show dog. In 1921, at a meeting held at Crufts Dog Show, the English Springer Spaniel Club, the parent club of Great Britain, was founded.

So far, twelve secretaries have done an excellent job. The longest serving - nearly twenty-five years - was the late Mrs Olga Hampton. The first seven secretaries were enthusiasts of the working dog.

This resulted in a good balance between work and show issues later on.

The Club is in good hands with an experienced committee. Two successful shows a year, a 22 class open show in April and a 34 class championship show in November, are organised. Each year a field trial sub-committee aims to run a novice and open stake.
The Club also organizes symposia and a video has been produced entitled 'Interpreting the Breed Standard'.

In total, there are eight English Springer Spaniel breed clubs in the UK. Membership to these clubs is subject to an annual fee and is open to anyone with an interest in the breed.

The English Springer Spaniel Club

Has section for the 'working' English Springer
Secretary: Mrs Y Billows
Tel: 01606 888303
Email: ess@robil.co.uk

The English Springer Club of Scotland

Has section for the 'working' English Springer
Secretary: Mrs K Simpson
Tel: 01337 830154
Email: kerry@revoviel.freeserve.co.uk

The English Springer Spaniel Club of Wales

Has section for the 'working' English Springer
Secretary: Mrs Heidi Turner
Tel: 01902 654629
Email: turner_edwin@hotmail.com

The Lancashire and Cheshire English Springer Spaniel Club

Secretary: Mrs J Demspey
Tel:01745 330088
Email: arngeirr@vikingsaga.fsnet.co.uk

The Midland English Springer Spaniel Society

Has section for the 'working' English Springer
Secretary: Mrs K Woodward
Tel: 01709 896 663
Email: wadeson@onetel.com

The Northern English Springer Spaniel Society

Secretary: Mrs N Calvert
Tel: 01609 772861
Fax: 01609 772861
Email: calvert@calvdaleess.freeserve.co.uk

The Southern English Springer Spaniel Society

Secretary: Mrs C Woodbridge
Tel: 01303 875 191
Email: crackerjanne@tinyworld.co.uk

The South Western English Springer Spaniel Club

Secretary: Mrs Janet Hawkins
Tel: 01452 555720
Email: janet.hawkins1@tesco.net

All eight societies are members of the Joint English Springer Spaniel Judging Consortium (JESS JC)

- A well brought up English Springer Spaniel is a pleasant companion. Make sure that you follow a puppy training course with your dog. It teaches both dog and owner a lot.
- Regularly feed your dog hard dry food and give it plenty of dog chews. This keeps your dog's teeth healthy.
- Never buy a puppy whose mother you weren't able to see!
- The English Springer Spaniel is an energetic dog. It wants to 'work' for its living, so ensure that you do plenty of things with it.
- Always ask to see the parent dogs' papers. Also ask about the results of checks for HD and of eye checks of both parents!
- An English Springer Spaniel is a good gundog. Bear in mind that a dog from a gundog line will often not be the easiest pet. It needs lots of exercise and plenty of challenges. Take this into consideration when choosing a puppy.
- Buy an English Springer Spaniel via a breed association.
- Do not let your puppy chase after a ball or stick endlessly.
- Never leave a dog alone with young children.
- Visit several breeders before buying your puppy.

Group:	Gundogs
Country of origin:	Great Britain
Original task:	Gundog
Present tasks:	Gundog, show dog, companion
Colours:	Liver and white, black and white, or any of these colours with a tan marking
Height:	51 cm (20 in)
Weight:	Approx. 32 kg (71 lb)
Character:	Friendly, happy, obedient and never aggressive or timid
Life expectancy:	13 to 15 years

The English Springer Spaniel

the **English Springer Spaniel**